# APPLES OF THE EARTH

P O E M S

*Dina Elenbogen*

S P U Y T E N   D U Y V I L
*New York City*

Cover art: Dedication to the music of Livaneli by Ilan Hasson

Author photo: Laura Friedlander

ISBN 1-933132-24-8

Library of Congress Cataloging-in-Publication Data

Elenbogen, Dina.        Apples of the earth : poems / Dina Elenbogen.

p. cm.        ISBN-13: 978-1-933132-24-2

1. National characteristics, American--Poetry. 2. United States--Poetry. I. Title.

PS3605.L38A86 2005                811'.6--dc22                2005020294

Acknowledgments

"A Jew in Vienna" was awarded the Miriam Lindberg Israel Poetry for Peace Prize. "Michigan Raspberries" was a recipient of the Three Oaks Poetry Prize. "Drought to a South African Friend" was a finalist in the National Writer's Poetry Competition judged by Adrienne Rich. "Climbing the Wall" was winnter of Voices Israel International Poetry Competition. "Say a Prayer but the Sea Wind Blows Them Out" is the text for an orchestral composition by Mark Engebretson, perfomed internationally. Grateful acknowledgment to the following magazines and anthologies where some of these poems first appeared, sometimes in earlier versions.

MAGAZINES
"Trains" "Jabotinsky Street"   Prairie Schooner
"Peeling Onions"   Calyx
"Say a Prayer" "But the Sea Wind..." "Blue Violet"    Poet Lore
"Leaving" "The Depression" "150 Years of Chicago Architecture"   Rhino
"Chilled Mulberries"   Primavera
"Apples of the Earth" "Waiting"   Shirim
"You Say Give Me Fire" "Distance Pantoum"    Seven Gates , Jerusalem
"The Fist and the Respite" "No Answers" "Climbing the Wall" "You Cannot Keep Love in This Country"
"Birthday Poem"    Jewish Women's Literary Annual
"Saul's Hammer"   Tomorrow Magazine
"Rising for the Buddha" "Freud's Chair" "Waiting"   Strong Coffee
"Climbing the Wall" "A Jew in Vienna"   Voices Israel


ANTHOLOGIES
"The History of Night"
Beyond Lament Northwestern University Press, Evanton, IL.
"The letter I Wanted to Write..." "Jabotinsky Street" "The Depression" "Saul's Hammer"
"The Last Person Out of the Country..."
Sarah's Daughters Sing: A Sampler of Poems by Jewish Women   Ktav publishers, New York.
"Ma'alot Cafe" "Apples of the Earth"
Without a Single Answer: Poems about contemporary Israel, Judah Magnes Museum Press
"Maybe it is Raining Today in Nebraska"
The American Dream   Pig Iron Press, Youngstown, Ohio.


With deepest gratitude to the Ragdale Foundation where during several different residencies some of these poems were born and brought to life, the Illinois Arts council for two fellowships and an award that supported the making of some of these poems and to Hilai, the artist's colony in Ma'a lot, Israel for shelter and space to create. .

*For my mother, Irene Kaplan Elenbogen*
*In Memoriam 1928-1998*

# CONTENTS

*I want to sing a psalm of praise to all that remains*
*here with us and doesn't leave, doesn't wander off like migratory birds,*
*will not flee the north or the south, will not sing "In the East is my heart,*
*and I dwell at the end of the West." I want to sing to the trees*
*that do not shed their leaves and that suffer*
*the searing summer heat and the cold of winter,*
*and to human beings who do not shed their memories*
*and who suffer more than those who shed everything.*
*But above all, I want to sing a psalm of praise*
*to the lovers who stay together for joy, sorrow and for joy.*
*To make a home, to make babies, now and in other seasons.*

Yehuda Amichai
from *Open Closed Open*

# I

*Large Gardens of a Strange America*

# ARID LAND

Everything hinged on
how many apples

landed in a basket
the way water was absorbed

by earth, the words that were
and were not spoken

once all the branches
were bare.

In the dream I remembered
what home was

that it had to do with gathering
our own fruit

sometimes with suffering
always with love.

We had managed to plant
in this arid land;

the darkness was about the grief
the land gave back.

The darkness was about forgetting
The dream of home.

In the room where my son fights
sleep, a squirrel ate through old wood.

We have filled the cracks
with cotton, sealed them with tape.

Below his window my daughter plants seeds
in the shade of Oak leaves.

We have let go the dream
of berries, asparagus and pears,

our trees have swallowed the light.
Sometimes, when we drive the crowded streets

of our lives, my young son points to open windows.
He says, *this could be our home.*

My daughter wakes me from this trance
and says, *I like where we live now.*

She leads me back to the garden
where white petals catch wind

lean east toward the other home
where dreams, too, were planted

where with enough tools
we could irrigate the soil

plant things and watch them grow.
Where we thought, with enough

plaster and paint we could cover
bullet holes in the roofs of ancient houses.

## MICHIGAN RASPBERRIES
*for Sarina*

The dreams you reach for
in these tall trees, bleed
on your three-year-old fingers.
The darkest and sweetest fruits
hang in high places, others
reach with ladders.

But together, in nearby fields, we can grasp raspberries,
stain our hands with red juice
you wipe on your white cotton dress
with flowers falling
past your scraped knees, and around us
nothing but flowers.

My young daughter, with lips as full
as this golden fruit, we stand here in the middle
of American fields, flat as the innocence
I will not steal by speaking just now
of those other fields
I almost claimed as my own.

In this other country I picked apples
in return for the holy tongue,
scraping my arms in high branches
our people claimed, land
others, too, have called their own.

Today, I want to be nowhere
else but in this moment of passing
raspberries, from my hands to yours
dropping them into buckets
and back from your hands to mine.

Dear one, these hands have grown withered
in these other fields, these other dreams
we cannot touch, not even
on the undersides of leaves.

# GROUND SHIFTING

When the ground we have been standing
on shifts, where do we plant our feet?

On either side of the ravine, weeds
with flowers only grow in the shade.

I would pick them but
I promised not to get in the way.

I did not ask for the shape of things
to change. On a crowded bus in Jerusalem

when someone tossed away
an apple core, everyone turned around.

I did not offer my seat
to the woman with seven sons.

I did not ask the veiled women
to offer you their silk.

I did not ask for the absence
of rain. I did not

mean to return
to a yellow earth.

I asked, only, to be loved
and to the ground I asked

when it shifts
not to bury me.

# Rising for the Buddha

Who falls onto the El with groceries for three
generations; who escaped pirates and prisons
to arrive in a place where a man
sees clotheslines of a different poverty
pass through a train window.
Who with wrinkles of sixty monsoons
lets a woman rise
from her seat for him
to replace her.
His fists are full with green onions
from the large gardens of a strange America
he takes home to a table
where everything and nothing
wait for him.

# In all this Heat We Are

Strangling our ankles with garden hose.
Water squirts in all directions, my black
skirt wraps around my legs, my left
breast is outlined in sweat.

Sometimes I cherish this soaking
the earth, bringing back
lilies, lettuce and phlox.
Other times I curse these chores:

weeds passing as flowers
swallowing everything that struggles
to bloom.

Across Lake Michigan Ibrahim
waters his hollyhocks. In the western light
they are ladders of flame
crimson, salmon, magenta—

each petal a step out
of the hell in which he has
found himself. Three seasons
behind bars. Out on bond.

Someone else may say the hollyhocks are taking over
but this watering, this spreading of color
has become his prayer, this bringing back
the smell of Michigan soil.

It is only reluctantly that he passes the hose
to the mother of his daughter,
to greet strangers who have come
to say *welcome home*.

He has not taken his eyes
off the place where water
hits earth. He breaks the small talk
to remind her not to forget
the dry patch in between stalks
as if everything depended upon it.

He has been called freedom fighter
refugee, citizen, restaurant owner.
He has been called lover, father, friend
son and brother.

He has lived in prison
these long months
a borrowed country trying
to right itself

A Patriot Act
An innocent victim
He has become victim.

Mother passes the hose
to their daughter. Her white shirt says
"Free my Dad." She has drunk injustice
like mother's milk, spills

water everywhere
squeals louder than the parched tongues
of Midwest snapdragons. She sprays until
his pant cuffs are wet

and all of us watching are covered
in water, drenched in laughter
that covers the silence, the dry patches
the strangers who don't know what to say

except don't worry
soon it will dry
in all this heat
we are

## THE LETTER I WANTED TO WRITE, THE LETTER I WROTE
### for Osnat an Ethiopian student in Israel

*In the Medinah, in Marrakech*
*a veiled girl tried to sell me a basket*
*she wove in greens, purples and the color of wheat.*
*Heavy lipped, black alabaster, like you*
*she stumbled through my language*
*pleading 20 dirham, 15 dirham . . .*

EVERYTHING IS FINE IN AMERICA.
I AM TEACHING AT THE UNIVERSITY.
I JUST GOT BACK FROM A VACATION FAR AWAY
NOT FAR FROM WHERE YOU WERE BORN.
YESTERDAY IT RAINED SO HARD
THERE WERE RIVERS IN THE STREETS.

*The veiled girl grabbed my wrist*
*with her slender fingers*
*chanting 10 dirham, 5 dirham . . .*
*When I walked away I saw your eyes*
*large wooden bowls, waiting*
*to be filled.*

ARE YOU HAPPY IN YOUR NEW COUNTRY?
ARE YOU STUDYING VERY HARD?
ARE YOUR BROTHERS AND SISTERS STILL WITH YOU?
DOES YOUR MOTHER FEEL BETTER
NOW THAT THE RAINS HAVE PASSED?
I AM SORRY. I CANNOT SEND MONEY.

*In the Medinah there were rugs*
*the colors of mountains and sky*
*and baskets in the bony arms of girls*
*like your thin legs that carried you*
*from Ethiopia to Sudan*
*and then to the place that was promised.*

HAS THE DREAM COME TRUE?
CAN YOU WRITE IN THREE LANGUAGES? SING
"BY THE WATERS OF BABYLON" IN ENGLISH?
I HAVE NOT STOPPED HUMMING THE WORDS.
MY STUDENTS ARE LEARNING POETRY
BUT DO NOT TAKE IT OUTSIDE THE ROOM.

*My students have golden pens.*
*They do not braid my hair in summer.*
*They run circles not knowing*
*of smaller countries*
*empty plates, washing in rivers*
*the sun asleep in fallow fields.*

DO YOU STILL WEAR THE BLUE BEADS
I GAVE YOU?
EVERYTHING IS OKAY IN AMERICA.
I HOPE YOU ARE WELL.
PLEASE EXCUSE MY LANGUAGE.
I HAVE ALMOST FORGOTTEN IT.

*I bought the basket from the girl*
*whose eyes shone through her white veil.*
*She wanted me to have another*
*but it was dusk*
*my arms were full*
*I pressed the coins to her palm.*

I AM SORRY.
I CANNOT SEND MONEY.
IT IS NOT EASY.
IT DOES NOT GROW ON TREES.
I PROMISE I WILL VISIT.
NEVER STOP WRITING.

*I filled the basket*
*with dirty clothes*
*and brought them back to America.*
*In the basement I hear them spin*
*and dream of rivers*
*cleansing orange against wheat.*

## DROUGHT: TO A SOUTH AFRICAN FRIEND

*for Cha*

You have written of the long drought
in Southern Africa
the rain that finally fell

on the white folks
who stood under colored umbrellas
the ones, unlike you, who believed

the rain was exoneration,
the ones who went home
forgiven and whole.

And I have not written
since Lake Michigan spilled over
since the city streets became rivers.

I have not written since the photos
you sent of a starving Ethiopia
the years without rain

the grain they carried
from one part of the country
to the other. I wept to hear

how in your own quiet way
you still fill your belly
like a ravenous animal

and then you empty
until your stomach is as flat
and forgiven as the land I live on.

In the Middle West of America
we are suffering, not dying
of thirst. Dead fish rot

on land that was water
last month. Our sinks are full
but the tomatoes we've waited for

all winter are slow to come,
our fruits will be sent
from someone else's soil,

        the fruit we waited for all winter.

It was a difficult winter.
Things tore at the seams,
things came apart slowly:

a knitted blanket unraveling
at the ends, water leaking
through the ceiling into buckets.

We emptied the buckets
and then they were filled.
We broke things and let them break:

a hand painted bowl
a blue pot from another generation.
We saw it all over each other's faces.

It was as if everything was taken
away and nothing replaced.
I don't know how else to tell you.

Things broke without remedies.
We didn't starve.
I know what you must be thinking.

Love survived in the middle of everything.
It is unlike the love
you describe.

The walls we built were small and made of stone.
Love filled our stomachs
but our hearts became clay.

Love grew in our bellies and our hearts
slowly became stone.
We fixed only what could be fixed with our hands.

Snow fell and we shoveled.
It was white and pure like in the postcard
of frozen rivers that I sent you.

And suddenly the sky stopped promising.
Spring lied. She turned right into the oven
of summer. She was more cruel than the lilac bush

and her tempting smells.
Secrets were kept and then given back.
The heart battled with the belly.

The way you starve yourself for beauty
and for hatred of the body,
we starved ourselves for love.

When love died the belly closed;
it refused to take anything in. The seeds
were gone, they had not been planted.

We turned to other crops
but there was no water
to help nurture them.

We starved ourselves because love left.
We did not think about Ethiopia.
Once we sent money.

Once we felt guilty for leaving
food on our plates.
I know it has been this way for you.

You have fasted during your own famine.

We cannot repair the broken bowls
from another generation.
We are making new bowls with our hands.

They are blue like the sky we once believed in.
We are polishing them and filling them
with the new expensive fruits.

They are sweet and we keep what we swallow.
The belly wins over the heart.
We stand with our hands open letting go.

It is our hands that let go
of stones, love
the fist.

We are waiting for rain
waiting for exoneration
from crimes we've committed on ourselves.

We are waiting for the sky, who has the final word.

# CHILLED MULBERRIES

I am empty of you.
Even the branches scratching
my window all winter have left
their gifts on my roof.

In the early hours
I collect the mulberries,
walk through the fallen
ones, crush them with bare feet.

If I could I would walk
all over your ceiling,
bring red
to your dreams.

A pregnant woman dreams
her own death. All night I dream
the loss of other people—
an old neighbor suddenly aged

and then his wife. A small animal
struck and buried. Then it is my mother
and I grieve remembering the lack
of inflection in her voice

long distance, my father eating alone
at dusk. I dream of bringing chilled
mulberries to everyone I love,
sweep the rest away.

# PEELING ONIONS

You loved to watch me undress
the onion, layer by layer.
Maybe it was me, removing your clothes
for the first time, or the children

we dreamed of under
too many layers of cloth.
You once said that for a small woman
I had a giant heart, like an ant

who had to be twice as strong
to carry a crumb on its back.
Have I been an ant building
a house destined to fall?

There are still things you don't know,
that as a child I slept with a fear
of hurricanes sweeping away my house
and a fear of making someone lonely.

That some nights I slept surrounded
by elephants and lambs, dolls without eyes.
That somewhere part of me still lives
in the yellow kitchen

where I sauteed onions and peppers,
where you made eggs with garlic
mornings when salt was not enough,
where I sat on your knees

making names for unborn children.
That tonight I peeled onions,
and when I threw away their tiny jackets
everything inside me wept.

# WAITING

I lean against a white wall
and study Monet's *Winter*.

And I know that somewhere
something falls that gently,

and there is a tree so covered
with snow and sky, it is blue.

In Monet's *Winter* there is a bridge
with no one waiting

at either end. I almost believe
in such peace.

# YOU CANNOT KEEP LOVE IN THIS COUNTRY

> *After love, the land*
> *After the land, nothing.*
> Miguel Hernandez

You cannot find love in this country;
it has slipped through your fingers
like the sand of a blistering desert,
has blown through your clothes
like the meanest Chicago wind
or you are sheltered from it
with the heavy green coat
a stranger once gave you.
She warned you to beware of the cold
and vanished with the first gust
of wind. You didn't want her
anyway. You only wanted the warmth
which she passed onto you.

You cannot keep love in this country.
It is more expensive
than your other dreams
more costly than the room
with four windows, or the city
with hot tubs where it is always sunny.
It costs more than the car you left in Haifa
and the apartment that belonged
to your grandfather, your father
then you.

You cannot treasure love in this country.
It is given to you with conditions
explanations, threats and demands.
It is more fragile than your mother's voice
over seas and mountains of wire.
It has danced in front of you
has pulled you down on your knees

has threatened your manhood.
It is heavier than the ammunition
you carried across deserts, hills and dunes.
It has screamed louder than gunfire
has threatened to suffocate you
like thick American pillows.

You cannot destroy love in this country.
It has asked for something back,
has threatened to leave as you pushed it away.
It nags at your spine, its voice constantly
in your ear, its green eyes the color
of the land where you have fallen.
You cannot destroy love in this country;
it refuses to let you sleep.

## II

If after love there is only land
and after land there is nothing,
what comes after that?
I have asked this in three languages;
it sounds most honest in words
that are not my own.
I have held onto love even after
it has died,  have tried to tell you
in your own language but you only listen
when I speak my own tongue.

I have stepped down from trains and believed
the stranger waiting was a man I once loved
on a train in your country. He left me
a red sweater for cold Jerusalem nights.
I believed he would know where to find me,
the exact corner of my city,
the moment of my departure.
I believed he had been waiting
all these years for something I once promised.

He smiles and looks the other way.
It is not he but a stranger waiting
as another woman steps down from the train.
I can no longer feel
the soil under my feet; it is still
frozen this early in March.
There is no place to plant trees
outside my window, we own nothing
not even air.

I cannot find land in this country,
land that is pure enough to love.
I cannot keep land in this country
cannot worship it in this hard city.
I cannot treasure land in this city
and so I leave and return
to the place you have left.

# II

## Apples of The Earth

# REACHING THE DESERT

From where you are you hike
one hour to reach the Dead

Sea, the sun setting over Mt. Masada.
My legs are strong from the hills

I climb to get home. It is almost
winter, darkness settles in my eyes.

Last month you gathered me
like wild flowers,

held me with both arms.
Today you learned to hold a rifle,

how to shoot. *Just in case*
you write from the desert, *not to worry.*

Through a cracked window I watch
squirrels store acorns in maple trees,

dream again of leaving.
In your country women fill baskets

with avocados, olives and bread,
fight the threat of Depression.

I miss you and your feet have
just reached the desert.

Today I want to feel the ache
in my legs, the harsh wind

inside my clothes, the near
miss of a car.

# DISTANCE

On my wall, a map of your country.
The headline says 48 Israelis wounded
In Jerusalem. Terrorist attack.
The scarf you sent wraps my neck twice.

The headline says 48 Israelis wounded.
Near the window I sip tea, smoke *Time*.
The scarf you sent wraps my neck twice.
I walk through the drizzle of another spring.

Near the window I sip tea, smoke *Time*.
Where you are the monsoon has ended.
I walk through the drizzle of another spring.
Mud must be drying on your boots.

Where you are the monsoon has ended.
You have learned to love a rifle.
Mud must be drying on your boots.
You say the map will bring us closer.

You have learned to love a rifle.
I have planted basil, tarragon and dill.
You say the map will bring us closer.
In *Sabra* the dead are silent.

I have planted basil, tarragon and dill.
In Jerusalem, terrorist attack.
In *Sabra* the dead are silent.
On my wall, a map of the country.


*Time* is a popular Israeli cigarette.
*Sabra* is a Palestinean refugee camp in Beruit where the brutal massacre of
1984 took place.

# No Answers

I want to know where the dead
rest in such a small country
and why with so many fallen
there is still room for apples.
Where are the men who walked
these groves with bare feet,
where is all the wine?
Do the dead rest,
do they wait?
My sleep here is different;
smaller things disturb me—
the opened mouths of wild dogs
birds carrying me somewhere else;
the harsh rhythm
of voices telling me
even in this ancient language
there are no answers.

## SAY A PRAYER, BUT THE SEA WIND BLOWS THEM OUT

You say it's easiest to embrace the dead,
easier to stand next to your grandmother's grave,
easier to light her a candle, toss a flower
across her eyes, easier to tell her why you must leave,
easier than your mother crying over dinner,
your mother with black wicked hair, your mother without
teeth. It is easier to turn your back on your grandmother's silence
then your mother standing at the doorway,
watching her oldest mistake walk away.
She throws stones at the moon which will not shatter.

You leave me with the heaviness of your grandmother
sunk in the earth of *Tarshiha*, where sheep pass
and the sun sets slowly behind white roofs.
You leave me with the spaces in your mother's mouth,
the darkness behind her eyes, the strap of her black
brassiere. You leave me with your father who has not spoken
since you threw him against the wall for hitting
your mother. His eyes are lost, his jaws clench
with each movement of your arm. You leave me with your father
selling *na'nna* on the street, the insufferable sun.

You leave me, my sun, alone on this bed we pressed
into, this narrow space you once shared with three
brothers and a sister. Then, there was only darkness,
reading books over candle. There are still things
I can't imagine. You leave me with the Breasts
of Ma'alot, the sun an orange ball, sinking past
the windmill, beyond the Arab villages, sinking
into the sea on one side of the sky, the moon up
on the other. You leave me with these heavy roads
that once were gravel. You leave me with your childhood
steps, your madness.

You leave me, walking alone past the shul
where you went as a boy with your skull-covered friends
and all of the other men pulled out of bed late night to pray.
It was the fruit you wanted, the cake you devoured,
this month before the Day of Atonement. I walk, still,
the staircase to your room. There is no light just
a few slats of open space to let the moon in.
You said once, the world is mostly darkness, that is why
we need these things: candles, menorahs and bulbs,
that is why you tell me just before the first three stars
appear to light the candles for the Sabbath.
I press them in the sand,
say a prayer, but the sea wind blows them out.

*Tarshiha* is an Arab village in the Western Galil.
*Na'nna* is mint leaves.
*Ma'alot* is a Jewish development town in the Western Galil.

When the news comes on
the parrot chatters like mad
from his cage, digesting each word
in his narrow throat, while I drink
tea with sheeba leaves, sweet wafers and time.
Twelve of us taken today,
just over the border.
I have come here from the school
where Ethiopian children can't learn
my language but repeat all the sounds.
Even in this fog a car starts up.
We've lost the view of mountains
but hear planes whiz by us
on their way to Lebanon.
When the news is over and the music
comes on the parrot is silent.
I return to school breathless.

## THE LAST PERSON OUT OF THE COUNTRY, PLEASE TURN OFF THE LIGHTS

The women, (hair wrapped in colorful scarves,
plastic baskets hanging from their wrists),
invade the market like hawks.
Tomorrow, everything doubles.
Bat Sheva gets enough toilet paper
to last until the next *Khamsin*, like all of us
buys her bread fresh each day.
I grab tomatoes with the least bruises.
Someone rushes off quickly to another city.
Our mail undelivered days.

Tomorrow the country just may close down.
The country is angry at itself
for the price of next week's meat
for the split party
for the black children with mismatched skirts
for the black children with skull covers
for the stones that are thrown at them
for the stones that were thrown at us
for the black children with different prayers
for the black children with extra skin
between their legs.
The country is ashamed of itself
for giving in
for not giving back
for the absence of cigarettes
on storefront shelves, between
lips, under tables, for the emptiness
between its fingers.

The whole country threatens to stop tomorrow.
The Hasidim will throw their prayer books at the flies
beggars will close their fists on Rabbi Kook street
buses will stop on the Hill of Evil Counsel

a man and a woman will pull apart
before finishing, a letter will stop
in the middle of the sea on the way
to someone's heart.
Tomorrow everything, the trees too,
will lie down in exhaustion,
everything except the wind
opening and slamming doors,
everything but the flies finding their way
back to us, everything but the flies,
devouring what is already lost.

*Ma'a lot 1985*

*Khamsin* is a hot desert wind.

# LEAVING

I have nothing else to tell you,
we finished all the bread,

even the hard part, the part
I break off and save.

The mountains have become my only sustenance
beyond a thin pane of glass

or a table with only two
tomatoes and all of the words eaten.


I awoke to the hills of Bethlehem
in the west, Jerusalem stone in the east

the land changing but never leaving
through fog, wind and windstorm.

On *Tu Bishvat* I planted a tree
between the two cities.

Almond trees blossomed;
the morning I left it rained.


Once I judged a city
by the colors of clothes hanging.

underthings waving to the sky
were like so many tongues praying.

Today there is nothing beautiful
about my own clothes leaning

above the street, nothing mystical
about their stains.


Once I judged a winter
by the layers of clothes taken off;


one night there were five
with the unwrapping of the scarf

from my neck. In my heart
I have never left that room.

In Jerusalem winter was warm
on the highest part of the mountain.


Now, through one window,
there is the golden stone

of Galilee hills,
to the east, the Ethiopians

shoulders covered in white
sheets, their graceful

bows upon meeting,
bows and kisses upon leaving.


Once I judged a woman
by the number of loaves she carried

on her head, a man
from the honesty in his hands.

Once I judged a life
by the rings around a single eye,


I said leave,
but leave with steps I can't hear.




*Tu Bishvat* is the Jewish Arbor Day

APPLES OF THE EARTH

*(In the Guest House Restaurant,*
*Kibbutz Ramat Rachel)*

I

Everyone else is peeling onions
and I can't stop crying, can't
remember what I dreamt last night.
Muhamad shows me his card, tries
to tell me he's a Jew, lists
all of the serious holidays.
Shoshana shows me which shelves
to clean, which soap. I lift
a frying pan from the darkest corner.
The rust on my palm says maybe
the last time someone fried an egg
was the day we captured Bethlehem,
or the month fifteen of us
never came home. It's peaceful now.
The rattling windows just mean a plane
passes faster than the speed of sound.

II

The Arabs are building another room.
The German guests eat strudel, the Koreans green
melon, the Americans eat without trays.
Tamarah sings in Spanish and Hebrew
about horses and rivers in Brazil.
Sarinah and I dream of ski lodges in Aspen
and Vermont while we pick mint leaves
for our tea. I cut to the core
of the apple, the toughest but sweetest part.
The others drink coffee black, two lumps of sugar.

## III

My hands are no longer my own.
How many potatoes have I peeled,
how many bruises have I carved
away, tossed in the bin.
In this language they are called
Apples of the Earth.
I sing the old songs and time goes quicker.
Amnon makes cat sounds.
Why doesn't someone let them in?
Doesn't anyone think the cats are hungry
just because they beg? Doesn't anyone think
I too want tea with *Na'nna* just because I didn't ask?


*Na'nna* is mint leaves.

# JABOTINSKY STREET

*for Robert Friend*

For the man who nurses
twelve cats, one without claws,
one voiceless, one with tunnel vision,
I bring pomegranates from the market
on Ben Yehuda Street.
Last month they were ripe on the tree
in front of my lover's house.

I bring him these fruits for tomorrow
when I will already be on my way
to another country.
Each seed is a blessing.
I try to believe each seed
is another year of his life.

His Arab housekeeper serves us fish soup.
Bread is constantly popping from the toaster.
We critique the flavor of seasoning,
compare it with last month's stew,
last month, when my skin wasn't so brown
when the wine didn't spin my head so,
when I wasn't so close to the border.

Between the soup and sherbet
we critique my poems, his jewels.
He has taken in another cat this month,
without a tail, with a loud cry,
as I have taken in a new lover,
a Moroccan without manners.

We finish the game of solitaire
he began before I arrived. He keeps
turning up the ace of spades,
the card of death, says it always falls
from his neighbor's balcony, lands on his lawn,
something he stumbles past
on his way to collect the mail.

The oldest cat lands on the bookshelf.
His limbs heal in this room
where Martin Buber once stored
his books, where my friend collects
the words of three generations, writes
the words of two countries,
and gives me black tea.
I gather the fallen pomegranate seeds
plant them in a pot outside his window and pray
things will not stop blooming.

# POMEGRANATES

*"Granada," Spanish for pomegranate also means small bomb.*
*"Rimone," Hebrew for pomegranate, also means grenade.*

This is not a field of pomegranates
but a grove of small bombs.

I know you have wanted me
to feel their unequivocal beauty

but in Granada when I held one in my palm
everything I touched became fire.

You want me to feel I have fallen
into a field of pomegranates

but in Jerusalem
they ticked on every corner

even if they didn't
explode.

# THE FIST AND THE RESPITE
*for my American Friends in Jerusalem*


In Jerusalem, where everyone is holding
something back: urine, stones, the fist
we set the breakfast table,
fill the bowls on the balcony
with strips of red pepper
plump purple grapes, salads from the East.

If we leave the bread out for more than a moment
it will harden.
You tell me this as I look over
to where a man releases himself in a bush.
The bread crumbles into our plates
like the view of the Old City glazed in heat.

Pouring sweet milk into black coffee
we move into your childhood,
the year everyone had outgrown
the pumpkin except for you,
how you cried all the way home
from the market.


*

I cannot go to the Arab market alone
anymore, you tell me, and only with someone
if we look and speak American.
Robert is wearing his cowboy hat.
Your arms are white and bare.
My legs are dark and covered to the ankle.

We buy music and flee,
don't go any deeper than we have to.
On the way out, herded together like sheep,
Robert mentions the fist in his back.
Someone is holding onto my waist.
You rage at the baskets of Arab women,
emptied by our soldiers, blood red
tomatoes staining the pavement.

After twenty years in Jerusalem,
yesterday Betsy threw her basket of fruit
into the air for no reason
and ran all the way home.

Today, in East Jerusalem, everything
closes at noon. In the shuk
the doors slam closed at two.
Yet we know that behind their iron gates
they still serve sweet tea
and stale bread.

No one mentions the stones being thrown
on the border, no one mentions the bullets
that are given back. No one knows if the hatred lives
in the land or in the heart.

                    *


In Jerusalem, where everyone is reaching
for something: love, money, food, salvation,
I bring you the most fragile flower I can find.

I bring Robert sweet white wine.
After thirty years in Jerusalem
he serves me chicken on a bed of salt.
We drink until I can almost not feel
the pain of all our bodies trying to find the quickest way out.

We edge along the wall
that has lasted centuries,
surrounds the whole Old City.
When there is a gate, we stumble
over. I don't know you anymore.
I swallow the distance
between this wall and the city below.
Even the skull-covered children beneath us
must wonder why a woman leans against a wall.
Tourists photograph us.
We've been here before and I keep wondering
how we've returned and why the Wall
looks the same from every angle.
I ask for your seed, for the desire
to become simple. You ask me to
photograph the way light hits
the long passage before us.

# III

## The History of Night

# TRAINS

1.
The first were childhood—
trains we made with chairs
when my mother lined them up
in the hallway, cardboard trains
in the doctor's office,
trains that led to Chicago.

When the train came up for air
among buildings, we would stare
into other people's windows.
I wanted to climb those rickety Chicago porches
with yellowing geraniums on the sill,
and always a cat perched on the ledge
where a window was missing.

When the train went below ground,
I remembered the red skin
of my next door neighbor, dying
of leukemia, and President Kennedy on T.V.
in a striped box, my parents
weeping soundlessly.


2.
In the city it was the stone
lions in front of the Art Museum
who called to us. In the gift shop,
I asked my mother for a train set
like my cousin had. She bought me
marionettes.

On State Street I fell in love
with a pink clock
in the window of Shapiro's Jewelers.
On the train, on the way home,
my mother flipped the clock over
to find its origins. *Germany.*
I promised not to tell.


3.
For weeks the pink clock ticked
with the rhythm of trains, shined
like a forbidden apple.
When my father saw the name
on the clock he said nothing,
but his anger lived in the walls
he painted, and the fences he built
around our house.

My father's anger was red.
When he bathed he drowned in it.
He wore his anger in his clothes.
When he laughed it waited on his tongue.
When he lay down it rose above his head.
My father did not sleep.

Those mornings I walked with red
boots, burning patches in the snow.
At night I'd lie awake to the sound
of train whistles like worn kettles
and my father sealing windows
so the rain would not enter
so the air would not escape.

4.

*"Mother, was it the insufferable wind?"*
To the others on the train
from Chicago to LA
she was nothing but a sack
of flesh. When she slept,
children stole pennies from her purse.

I counted the numbers on her arm
like birds, added, subtracted,
until I knew there was no pattern.
When I told the others about the fire
and brand of order, their eyes grew
with the stars we watched
outside the window. In the morning
we picked purple violas that grew
near the tracks and placed them
in the buttonhole of her sweater.

5.

Years later, from Haifa
to Tel Aviv, I sat on a train
near a soldier who dreamed out loud
of a father who fell
against a barbed wire fence.
Ariel dreamed even in his waking. He said,
*Outside of this land we have nothing
but enemies.*

Later, we walked through Tzvat,
artists' colony, birthplace of Kabbalah.
I ran my fingers through rugs from Acre,
dresses from Brazil.
I stood listening to the ticking
of the beautiful German clocks

until the sun set and everything closed
around us.

We climbed above Tzvat
where trains didn't pass.
I tried to photograph the shadows
the sun left in the sky, until
Hassidic boys invaded us like hawks
with beards and kepot on their heads.
They threw stones at our backs.

Ariel whispered, *They don't like cameras
on the Sabbath.*
When they left, talking was difficult
so we gathered stones, like the mystics
on their knees gathering sparks.
Ariel threw them at the sky.
I threw them down the mountain
where I knew trains
would always pass.

"Mother was it the insufferable wind?" Galway Kinnell from
*The Avenue Bearing the Initial of Christ into the New World.*

# THE DEPRESSION

I

Bees celebrate Indian Summer
flying in and out of the window.
It's the beginning of the month
and the kitchen is almost empty.
We've been eating dark tuna all week.

Even the cat can't stand the heat.
She sniffs the floor for crumbs
and catches bees in her mouth until they go mad
or die. Their relatives pay no attention
to history, but it's too hot to close
the window with potatoes baking in the oven.

A friend once told me a person could live
on potatoes only if he ate enough of them.
But my friend wore a striped suit and shiny shoes
into Chicago every morning and added up
other people's bills. I laughed. Potatoes.
I still laugh.

It's easy to forget and buy jugs of wine
and shiny knives that are guaranteed
to cut through almost anything. It's easy
to forget until thunder rattles the windows
and the lights flicker and go out.

In the morning the paper is too wet
to read. It is easier to live outside
the world, ignore the bills in the mail,
hide in the darkness of shadows.

II

In the shadows of these walls, I see
my mother's hazel eyes at nine. It is
1939. She is alone in an apartment
much smaller than this one. My grandparents
are downstairs running the store they live above.

Her brothers and sisters are out with friends.
Dinner will be late tonight.
After awhile hunger just goes away. My mother
watches the potatoes browning in the oven.
The warmth feels good.

It isn't always this lonely. At night
there are eight of them sleeping across
the livingroom floor. My grandmother is too tired
to yell about my mother's only doll who emigrated
to the roof, or the dead field mouse the cat
brought home. No one took it away.

It is almost winter
so everyone will sleep close tonight
as if there were room for some sort of love.
Next week my grandfather will get more wood.
There is no room to worry about saving
on a crowded floor, except in the crevices
of the wall where the cat hid the other half
of the mouse for breakfast.

III

My mother never worried about the past.
She worried about sleeping through the night
without the sound of someone
else's dreams keeping her awake.
Of course there were dreams.
At night they flew above my mother's head
and she wrote them down on pieces of paper.

Late in the afternoon, while other families
sat down to eat, she threw the pieces
of paper inside the last sparks of fire.
At night, when she slept, they flew
out the chimney and danced
all over Chicago.

Her dreams didn't leave.
When I was a child she would rock me in her lap
and read me stories about Adam and Eve,
how the world began. She fed pieces
of the past to me every night and they grew
in my sleep.

I remember how Adam cried on his first day
on earth when suddenly it got dark.
He thought G-d was taking the world away from him.
Adam didn't know the sun would come back
if he closed his eyes and rested,

the way my mother closed her eyes
and waited for the space to breathe,
the way I close my eyes and wait for the lights
to come back on.

Yehuda Leib was shot by Cossacks
in broad daylight
in front of his wife, simply
for being a Jew.
Saul was a Socialist, in prison
then working in the fields
and in the book.
Angry and aimless he came and stayed
in America, but failed
to pray like his father.

My father carries his fathers' demons
from sleepless rooms
to glasses of brandy to hot baths
to dusk filled streets
on his white bicycle, alone
at 65, his wife asleep
until sun-up.

My father's father's words kept him
from being lonely in the war.
I have prayed to words and to water.
I don't know what words to give my father.
I don't know who the fighters are
in his war. We cycle sometimes
in silence through fields.

Ten years ago I wrote the words
"I am tired because
he has not slept."

While sleeping in his house
I dreamt him walking circles
through black rooms.
I stepped out into what I thought

was his darkness
but instead I walked into my own
reflection in the mirror.

The terror of my own self
coming towards me
was a deep scream that awakened
my father, it came from the deepest part
of my throat.

It said
I don't know how to keep us
from being lonely

It said
I don't know how to live
with our demons or our dreams

It said
I don't know how to keep us
still

It said
I am living in stillness
with my demons and my dreams

It said
I love you through three
generations and six lifetimes

It said
I will never lose this terror
and I will never lose this love.

# SAUL'S HAMMER

Today it matters, that I hold
this hammer in my fist, that maybe
fifty years ago you held this hammer
in your fist, that I know this only
because your name is engraved in the metal.

So I call this hammer Saul, and Saul
hangs calendars, plants, and baskets
of bananas, oranges, and onions.
That Saul escaped Russia, was a Socialist, fixed teeth,
had the purest white hair at the end of his life—

these are only stories; that you died
when my mother's belly was full.
There are other things
I would have never asked you:
how you felt when you saw the first

buds on a tree, or the last,
that you never had time to notice
the blossoming or the dying
and what that meant.

*Saul Katzenellenbogen  1877-1953*

# GATHERER OF INJUSTICES

Libby gathers all of the injustices
and saves them to tell another generation:
the year no one would replace the button
that fell from her only leather shoes
(the ones that covered her ankle,
the ones that everyone wore)
how she went to the shoe-maker alone
with the quarter she was saving for the movies
how he sewed on a new one
and since she had no English
to thank him or to apologize,
she ran out with her long Russian braids
flapping behind her in triumph and in shame.

1920 comes back to her with the love
no one gave her
not her brother-in-law turned father
who brought her to this country
who raised her and disapproved of her
and sent her to work in the factory
who lay dying one night when no one had time
to take her further than the street car . . . .
The year Gil, her favorite nephew asked her not to
marry Dave who lived on a shelf
on Maxwell Street.
How she married him anyway
and in their loveless union brought three sons
(who have all drifted) and one daughter
into a crumbling relentless city.

Libby wears all of the small injustices
in her wrinkled but graceful face;
she shares them with her grand nieces
and with her best friend Bertha, a little less green
a little less angry, not unlike school girls
they reminisce in hushed voices—

how sweet the children were before they grew up
how beautiful they were in the lacy dresses
she gave them when she didn't have a penny
for herself, how quickly they grew
out of them and forgot . . .

And Libby remembers Gacey and the small boys he buried
under his suburban garage, and the man who killed
all of those nurses (she wishes death upon them all.)
She can't believe how her dreams, their dreams,
the country's dreams, have turned
into darkening, crumbling, Chicago alleys.

She does not mention the other injustices:
her sister who went to buy fresh rolls
from the bakery on Lawrence early one morning
and was shot, eight months pregnant.
She does not mention her family who stayed
in Russia and was killed, all of them
or her brother Leo who came on the boat with her
who was raised in an orphanage in Chicago
until he became a man
and Hitler gained power in Germany
Franco in Spain
until he flew to Cordoba to fight Fascism
and fell in his first battle
where 40-something years later
his great American niece eats overpriced pollo
and gaspacho next to Maimonides' birthplace
while all of her things are taken.

But these are not Libby's memories,
the gatherer of injustices:
the soda given to her grand niece
instead of her daughter
the invitations that stopped coming
as the generations multiplied
the sabbaths broken

the hissing of dry heat
that took up the silence that was
her dead husband, may he rest in peace
(let them all rest in peace. . . .)

What do the children and their children do
when she hands them her injustices
grown larger over time? They are married
to the unanswerable ones.
They write poems, study history,
marry for love or do not marry.

They bring her flowers but she does not
put them in water—they make her sneeze.
She tosses them, frowns, holds the Kinder close
and cooks whitefish with tomatoes
like their grandmother, her sister did
when she was alive. They come back
for second helpings because she is all
that is left of a distant world,
the rhythm of her voice is all
that is left of an ancient language
a precious language of injustice and beauty.

# HOLY CITIES
*Sept. 2001-Dec. 2004*

This is not Jerusalem
but the Avenue of the Americas
where my bag is searched on the way
in and out of the public library,
the one where lions sit
on Fifth Avenue, just north or south of Forty-Second.

And it is not Jerusalem but Chicago
where I remove my boots
with metal zippers, where my young son
takes off his hush puppies and runs
through detectors, in this land of the brave
and the free.

In the sky, between two American cities
my daughter asks if I'm afraid
when our plane hits clouds.
I say no, swallow terror
deeper than sky.


My daughter was born at the end
of the millennium and she questions
always, the beginnings of things.

My son was born at the beginning of the century
and words come to him, slowly.
Before he learned **plane**
he saw a sky change
saw a day in America

where nothing rose up
and nothing landed. Where birds
announced the day.

Is there a place in this poem
to utter something as unfathomable
as a plane into buildings?
It drags the line.
Buildings. Planes. Poems.
Beginnings. Life. Endings.
A generation that
speaks slowly
carries big sticks.

We bow down
remove our shoes
open our bags
where
every city has
become holy.

# IV

## Shattered Stone

## There is a Large Stone on the Path

There is a large stone on the path
to remind you where to turn back
to the house you were born in.

Even if you are walking aimlessly
even if you are guided by cat-tails,
lupine, rare prairie plants . . .

You will find that even the straightest path
turns inward, circles back
to that one unmoving stone

turned monument
with someone's father's name
to remind an aging poet

that her father built her
a house of wood that has stood
the harshest prairie storm

years with the attic left open
during heavy rains
history dampening in sealed trunks.

The stone bears every grandfather's name
the man who married your grandmother
who built a house your mother had to leave

a house with stones leading to the entrance
shattered stones you stumble over
no matter how far you think you've come.

*Ragdale House, Lake Forest, IL*

# 150 Years of Chicago Architecture

In demolishing the buildings,
we see how they were made,
how many years of wind
and water, what they carried
inside themselves.
From the patterns in door knobs
the winding of steps,
we can guess what year it was,
what people wore, if they undressed
in the light or dark.

When you take off my clothes
you cannot see my heart.
When you try to push
all the way inside
you cannot see my past—
but when you make it so I cannot breathe
or let go, you can see
with what fragile pieces I was made,
how easily I come undone.

I want to live in a house built long after the fire.
I want the old smells of rain held captive,
mildew and dust. I want a giant willow
to weep over my house in autumn,
a corner where even my bravest son
would be afraid to hide.
I want wood so solid
it can't be stripped
except to discover Jacaranda
underneath.

# You Say Give Me Fire

You say give me earth
and I dig around the long roots
of a tree, I dig until there is earth
inside my nails. Can you keep
what lives inside me
without losing everything
you own?

You say give me air
and I take you
to an icy bridge. There is snow
falling around us. It laces
my hair, lands on my tongue. You say
give me air and we walk until the bridge
seems to lean into the river.

You say give me water
and I say it might ice.
You say give me water
and I skate on the river until
it cracks. I gather pails full
of water, I gather until my hands
freeze—you promised to follow.

You say give me fire
and I say we are both fire.
You say give me fire, I
gather twigs and stone,
I light a match to everything I own, we
watch the fire laughing until it burns out.
The ashes? They live inside.

# FREUD'S CHAIR

You say it looks like Freud's chair
the wooden rocker in the corner
where the cat stretches as I peer
into other people's windows.

You call it Freud's chair
the chair where you do puzzles
while I bake bread, where you ignore
my poems and my suggestions.

It has come to look like Freud's chair
the chair where I tell you of people
who don't touch anymore, my friend who believes he's Moses
the snakes around my ankles.

We call it Freud's chair
the chair we sit in
not smoking pipes, the chair
we sit in sharing dreams,
the chair we sit in telling lies.

# SECRETS

When I rode past you today, as if I had never
seen you before, I was on my way to a quiet place
to read my students' secrets.

I ask my students to invent half-truths,
embellish other people's lies
the unmentionable dream.

I ask them to write their forbidden
words on scraps of paper,
to fold them neatly,

place them in the cap
of the only man in the room,
to reach in and choose

someone else's lie
to build a bigger lie on it
to build a poem.

They hate walking into someone
else's glass house; they want their own
shards of glass

their own sad stories.
They don't know how
to imagine other people's lies.

\*

I tell my lover to have never betrayed
is a sign of weakness.
I have books full of secrets.

I have told him
of unanswerable loves
and how I fear

the prison bars of unconditional
love, the absence of rain
the missing piece

the sudden touch of a hand
the quiet place after love
the silent place after love.

*

My students are at their desks
re-writing other people's secrets,
counting syllables on their fingers.

I fear the lives built
around the suburban lawns
I see from this window.

I fear this quiet and static
love. I tell these poets:
*secrets are meant to be given away.*

Yet I am comforted that only you
and I know that I rode past you
and your baby in the park today.

I was pedaling to forget.
I was pedaling away my darkness.
I was treasuring my one hour alone.

I was looking at a young woman
with black hair, two red lips
shiny for a day in the park.

I was looking at a woman
who could have strolled
through Seurat's day in the park,

a woman who sat before her reflection
hours, before she stepped out
into the world that is her stage.

When I saw in a split second
that it was your face
I looked into

I kept on pedaling
not breaking my rhythm
for a moment

even after you called my name
in a flat unquestioning tone
as if to say aloud

we have become strangers
in a park next to the lake
where we told secrets

as waves turned to years
and then decades—
I pedaled past

the fires we built as one year
changed into the next
where we dreamed of men

who would have us
and protect us
and let us be—

past your performances
where I sat with your lover
and left with him

before the play was over.
I never told you he kissed me
on the lips and I let him

although that was the place
I stopped.
I rode past the years

you stopped returning
calls, the years you stopped dreaming
and my dreams unnerved you.

I rode past the years I judged you
too harshly, the years there wasn't enough
time for secrets.


Today you are still beautiful
in the sun near the water,
freckled like a girl.

No one knows I would not stop
to hold your daughter
the way you didn't stop

to tell me, at last
your belly was full, that you
made something you could keep.

I did not stop to tell you my life
is intricate like lives
we imagined,

that my dreams live
next to me in sealed books,
while my lover and I sleep

next to the sound of water turning
water
against stone.

*

My students have finished
re-writing their secrets.
I return to them

as if I had not
just come back
from the untelling of my own lie.

# SYLVIA

Your daughter was born in London
the same day I was born in Chicago
to first generation Americans.

At two she watched you hang white
sheets in the English countryside
erase words as quickly as she formed them.

While my mother steamed creases
from my father's cotton trousers
I searched wooden boxes for letters

with magnets, formed them
into sounds on the green board
that hung in the basement.

I told my mother I hated
that we were English; she assured me
we are more than our language.

We are Americans.

You had a second child.

Your children asked for things
with English accents
watched you stand near water

wondering if you could reach
the other side.
Their faces brought you back.

My mother stayed in the world
until I gave birth to a daughter
and then she left gracefully, alone.

You sealed your children's room
so the gas wouldn't reach them.
Maybe you said goodnight

or maybe you left nothing
but words, unruly travelers
begging to come home.

# FOUR OF US DIVIDED INTO TWO CANOES

*Lake MacBride, Iowa*

Yashen says not to talk
just to listen.

Yael and Yitzhak make splashes
that sound like laughter.

Canoes tied together
with damp shirts,

we dive out of our boats.
Yael and I call to each other

in another language. To the others
it seems we've drifted far.

This water is different
because when we swim without

shirts, the fishermen can't
see our breasts,

and when we swim away,
our boats wait for us.

Yashen and Yitzhak hide
under a capsized boat.

Yael holds onto her orange
life preserver, dreaming

of Portland, looking out
to Russia. I swim the breast stroke

trying to make a perfect heart
with my hands.

This water is different
because when we look across

we see the same trees
and summer houses from every angle,

because we can feel its beginning
and its ending, like the poems

Yitzhak reads to us, like the rusted
hooks of the fishermen,

like their small limp fish,
like the oars that sliver

in our hands, like our lives
together.

# Maybe it is Raining Today in Nebraska

## I

Maybe it is raining today in Nebraska.
Maybe the house where you were born
is filled only with your father
roaming from room to room
his eyes half closed
when he sinks into his chair.
I don't know if he was dreaming
when he awakens with his cigar
loose between his lips.
It is winter and the greenhouse
windows are laced with ice.
Forget the rain.
Let's say it is snowing today in Nebraska.
African violets are blooming pink, purple, and white.
It will be months before the crocuses,
hours before your mother returns home.

## II

I sit across from your father
at a table in Chicago.
Although he says nothing
he has the last word.
He has taken your mother's hand
has become a small boy, and you
a smaller one. You do not take
my hand or touch me.
It is forbidden to desire
across the table.
Your mother's eyes say, *No one is good enough
for my son although she is a nice girl.*
You have grown up in those words.

### III

Your father walks with his head
slightly bowed the way you do.
You still call him "Doc".
Near the lake, when the wind blows
through our coats, he says,
"Al Capone can keep this city."
He wants you to come back to Nebraska
back to the earth
where he grows cucumbers for pickling
tomatoes, zucchini and squash.
You still follow his recipes.
He wants you back when he rests
his hand on your shoulder, whispers
*These are the hands that diapered you.*

### IV

I take you to my parents' house
when they are away.
You have already seen my father, at Passover
proud beneath the painting of his father.
I bring you to the shelves
of stories I was told as a child,
the worlds I grew up in.
I take you to my room.
A photograph of myself at five
watches you touch me
as I laugh like adolescence.
Even as you love me I have gone back
twenty years.
The sobbing afterwards is about that passage.
It is for the shapes and heaviness
of the leaves on the plants in my room.

It is for the way things keep growing
and decaying even when I'm away.
It is for the words my father gave me—
what to do with the house
if they never come back from their trip.
I mourn for the slowness of your father
before I come to know him,
the way your mother's pace speeds up.
I mourn that there is no comfortable place
for us to be.

V

I have loved you in Spain
when all of our clothes were taken.
I have loved you in Morocco
where veiled women called me your wife.
I have loved you in Portugal
where the sea brushed in loud sighs
all morning, where at dusk
the fishermen went home
to their ruddy-skinned wives.
I have loved you at the end of the world
where Columbus first looked
toward America.
I have walked with you through dead leaves
and have not felt you
have walked with the world swelling inside
and have had no words to tell you.

VI

You have seen my words through a microscope
the way you look at disease.
I have seen your heart change
from city stone to soft earth, have seen you weep
like a boy, have wanted to save you
from the world without me.

I have feared mornings in Chicago
the moment we cross
at different corners, the dull
gray of winter sky.


## VII

You have never taken me to Nebraska.
I don't know how hard
the rain falls in between your father's dreams,
if he will gather the crocuses in vases
or watch the petals cover earth.
I don't know if once your hand reached
into the soil, or if the soil touched
your lips. I have never tasted
what your father planted in Nebraska.

# BIRTH-DAY POEM
*for Steve*

The mother-in-law whom I will
never know glows on our table
each winter and now, so many years
later, her mother joins her in summer.

I have stood with you
over their places in earth and sky,
have wanted to give back to you
everything you have lost.

What does it mean when a mother
buries her own daughter, when a son
loses two mothers, brings his legacy
of loss to the woman he loves?

*

You want to walk the short path
toward your future, not the long aisle
where you would turn away
from your mother

toward me, the woman
who will be your wife.
You want to walk straight
to the chuppah, straight

to the future without closing
the door to your childhood
room, where no one
took anything away.

Your mother will not be there
to tell me how difficult
it can be to live
with your silence

how easy it is to love
you. Her silence has become
your prayer, her recipes
yellow in the cupboard, her meals

rise in the ovens of everyone
who ever loved her. I will
never keep you as full as she had,
will fill you instead with words.

What would your mother say
about the woman you chose
to be your wife?
If she had stayed all the way

into your manhood, would
you be so fragile?
Would sorrow stand
in the doorway of every joy?

It is almost your birthday.
This year it falls on the Sabbath.
You want to stay home, with me.
You don't want cake,

not even your mother's recipe.
You don't want friends
to join us, or family.
As if you want to mourn

your coming into the world,
as if you want to mourn
the long walk
you have had to take alone.

When we stand together, facing East
the lonely walk will be over.
You will break glass under your foot
to remember the sorrow, but from our palms
we will drink each other's joy.

# A Jew in Vienna

### 1. *Winter*

We come together sleepily, somewhere
between our time and theirs.
It is almost the end
of the year, the end of the millennium.
Other times, it is 1943,
the middle of the war.

*What is it we have*
*tried to create*
*in the birthplace*
*of the Fuhrer?*

My father dropped bombs
on this city when he was nothing
more than a child.
At 18 he went to war.
The war that ended in 1945 did not end
in my father's heart.

I don't know if the nausea I feel
this morning is a life slowly being formed
or my father's hatred reminding me
that nothing can grow
where something has been destroyed.

\* \*

Young Austrian men make music
to my poem of Jewish suffering.

Before they perform I read poems to closed
faces. I am introduced in German
and I don't understand anything but my name.

I do not slow down to let them enter
my language, only my landscape,
my Israel, my Middle America.

Something larger than all of us,
emerges beyond the veil of language.
I hear it in Catrina's voice.
On a small stage in Austria she sings
a Moroccan family breaking
in a border town in Israel

the voice that brings pain,
the violins that weep history,
the world that is so small
brings it larger, larger until it fills
the room, until it belongs, for a moment,
to all of us.

*What was your father doing during
the war.* My father bombed your city.
*What was it you said that your father
did?*


2.


*What was your father doing during the war?*
I never asked him this with anything more
than maybe my eyes but he answered me...

My grandfather wasn't well. He had a breathing
condition and so he couldn't serve...

And my father was too young or else he would have...

And I wasn't born yet but if I had been
I would have because that's just the way it was...

Christophe wanted to make music
to my poem of earth, air, wind and fire.

When we finished our coffee he walked
me to the subway. He assured me I'd know
my way back, that I wouldn't need a train.
He was in a hurry to catch his train.

He said he understood my poem but I didn't think
he knew anything about me so I couldn't tell him
the world had become unrecognizable
that as the sun that had never really risen, set
Vienna was a wasteland.

He said I was only blocks from my hotel
but I didn't know anything in the winter dark.
The streets had become lies, paths of deception.
Every corner I turned led me back to my terror.

Even the coins had changed so that
I had to ask a woman selling flowers
to help me call my hotel.
On the phone my husband told me
to describe where I was but I didn't
know how to tell him I'd entered
a kind of hell so I just said

there are flowers, frozen flowers
in huge vases and all of the gates
are slamming closed.

He told me which track to stand next to.
I could no longer feel my hands.

I stood shivering next to the green
line as people boarded and descended.
A woman going nowhere trying to get home.

When my husband appeared from nowhere
and threw his arms around me, he almost
brought me back to our world....
He led me to the room where I sat
under covers, drank cup after cup
of black tea but the cold wouldn't leave
my bones.

No more composers, I said.
Weeks later, in Jerusalem, I bled.


3. *Spring*

Put your hands on this round belly.
It is a globe of my world.
Inside the voice that rises when I sleep
asks for peace. It has not learned
of boundaries and borders. It remembers
everything I've tried to forget. Its starvation
is indistinguishable from my own.

I don't know if I will walk hand in hand
with a curly-haired son who one day
will protect me from myself....
Or if I will wrap a young girl's hair into braids
that will unravel slowly like my face
next to hers in the mirror.

What does this unborn child make of my dreams?
The voices of everyone I've ever loved
visit us in our sleep. Those who I have betrayed
want no revenge. Those who have betrayed me are leaving
pages of apologies outside my door.
I am afraid the wind will take everything away.

We who stop loving others more than ourselves
are those who have lost too much.
Those who have lost mothers and countries
dig a hole in the earth. We plant trees. We pray
for rain. We pray and we pray for rain.

I have feared losing this child days
after the seed was planted. I imagined the new life
did not want to take root, did not sit right
in my body, pushing to get out of this difficult world,
struggling to find a place to rest these long months.

How do I tell my child who understands
everything and nothing that I have always been at war
like the world I invite her to live in. And I have done nothing
to change it except live between words and silence

country and mother-land
forgiveness and letting-go.
I put my hand on my round belly and dream
of forgiveness so my child can sleep peacefully.
I dream of loving with everything I know,
everything we've lost,
everything we've tried to forget.

# A Year's End

It is quiet at this year's end.
Winter whispers through heavy coats.
I lace your boots. You catch your finger
in my loose curl.

The prairie isn't white
like we imagined.
Through dead leaves we see
a hidden sun, lost mitten
the drawbridge we scaled last summer.

You are six and know the language
of distant fields, the sudden surprise
of purple branches
praying to ice.

You have come to know the beauty
in what has been lost:
the way your hair curled at three
the child you were before you learned
the names of things—

the woman I was before
I carried you through three seasons
then set you free
before winter.

*

The waves turn toward a season's
end: pink sky, snow remnants.
The shore holds the place
where water turns back.  You've found a shell;
just as quickly you let it go.

Wet sand covers our boots.
I've folded the stray curl inside my hat.
Your laces make thin trails back
from sacred places.

Land, sky and shore touch
the force of December waves.
This is how a page turns
a year ends
a mother loves.

DINA ELENBOGEN'S poetry and prose have appeared in numerous literary magazines and anthologies. She has received fellowships and awards in poetry and creative nonfiction from the Illinois Arts Council and she is the recipient of the Miriam Lindberg Israel Poetry for Peace Prize. She has completed a book-length memoir *Drawn from Water: A Question of Home.*

Elenbogen has an MFA in poetry from the Iowa Writer's Workshop and teaches in the University of Chicago Writers' Studio. She lives in Evanston, Illinois with her husband Steve Siegel and their children Sarina and Ilan.

# S P U Y T E N   D U Y V I L
*Meeting Eyes Bindery*
*Triton*

WATCHFULNESS    Peter O'Leary

WALKING AFTER MIDNIGHT    Bill Kushner

WEST OF WEST END    Peter Freund

WHEN THE GODS COME HOME TO ROOST    Marc Estrin

WHIRLIGIG    Christopher Salerno

WHITE, CHRISTIAN    Christopher Stoddard

WITHIN THE SPACE BETWEEN    Stacy Cartledge

A WORLD OF NOTHING BUT NATIONS    Tod Thilleman

A WORLD OF NOTHING BUT SELF-INFLICTION    Tod Thilleman

WRECKAGE OF REASON    (ed.) Nava Renek

THE YELLOW HOUSE    Robin Behn

YOU, ME, AND THE INSECTS    Barbara Henning

Made in the USA
Monee, IL
07 July 2026

56544784R00080